Every good and perfect gift is from above.

JAMES 1:17

D0338661

Sunday, 05/13/'18

Antelope California

my 1st Mother Day in Antelope
with my family..... So happy

← The one of Most Beautiful gift that
I've ever received

A GIFT FOR:

Mom/Grandmom

FROM:

Johnette & Mom (Teresa)

05/15/18

"I've rather be Hopeful & Wrong,
than Hopeless & all right. - Savannah
Guthrie: Today's Show

Copyright © 2016 Hallmark Licensing, LLC

All scripture taken from the HOLY BIBLE NEW INTERNATIONAL VERSION®. NIV®.
Copyright 1973, 1978, 1984 by International Bible Society. Used by permission of
Zondervan.

Published by Hallmark Gift Books,
a division of Hallmark Cards, Inc., Kansas City, MO 64141
Visit us on the Web at Hallmark.com.

All rights reserved. No part of this publication may be reproduced,
transmitted, or stored in any form or by any means without the prior
written permission of the publisher.

Editorial Director: Delia Berrigan
Editor: Kim Schworm Acosta
Art Director: Chris Opheim
Designer: Laura Elsenraat
Production Designer: Dan Horton
Contributing Writers: Ellen Brenneman, Linda Barnes, Keely Chace,
Renee Daniels, Linda Elrod, Jake Gahr, Cheryl Hawkinson, Diana Manning

ISBN: 978-1-63059-004-8
BOK2290

Made in China
0916

YOU ARE A BLESSING

Hallmark

WHEN I THINK OF ALL
THE BLESSINGS
GOD HAS GIVEN ME,
I ALWAYS THINK
OF **YOU**.

Every good and perfect gift is from above.

JAMES 1:17

LOOKING DOWN
ON PEOPLE
ISN'T YOUR THING.
BUT WALKING
ALONGSIDE THEM
DEFINITELY IS.

Lucky me.

THERE MAY BE TIMES
WHEN YOU'RE AFRAID
TO DO WHAT'S RIGHT,
BUT THAT DOESN'T STOP YOU
FROM DOING IT.

I can do all things through him who gives me strength.

PHILIPPIANS 4:13

YOUR LIFE

TELLS A BEAUTIFUL,
ONGOING STORY
OF PURPOSE, COMPASSION,
AND WALKING IN FAITH.

AND EVERY NEW CHAPTER
JUST GETS BETTER AND BETTER.

"For I know the plans I have for you,"
declares the Lord,
"plans to prosper you and not to harm you,
plans to give you hope and a future."

JEREMIAH 29:11

YOU HAVE A
REAL GIFT
FOR UNDERSTANDING PEOPLE.
YOU SEE THEM
HEART-SIDE OUT...
THE WAY THAT
GOD
MUST SEE THEM, TOO.

YOU SEE
LIFE'S CHALLENGES
NOT AS STUMBLING BLOCKS,
BUT AS BUILDING BLOCKS OF
YOUR FAITH.

Consider it pure joy, my brothers and sisters, whenever you face trials of many kinds, because you know that the testing of your faith produces perseverance.

JAMES 1:2-3

YOUR OPEN HEART
AND CARING SPIRIT
ARE LIKE GOD'S SIGNATURE,
HIS THUMBPRINT, SAYING,
"This is a child of mine."

KINDNESS

FROM OUT OF THE BLUE...

THAT'S JUST SO YOU.

Be kind and compassionate toward one another.

EPHESIANS 4:32

YOUR JOY
IS THE KIND
OF CONTAGIOUS
THAT'S GOOD
TO CATCH.

A happy heart makes the face cheerful.

PROVERBS 15:13

YOU MANAGE TO
LOVE PEOPLE
EVEN AT
THEIR MOST UNLOVABLE.
NOTHING SHOWS
GOD'S LOVE
BETTER THAN THAT.

I LOVE SPENDING SOME FACE TIME WITH YOU!

I hope to see you soon, and we will talk face to face.

3 JOHN 14

YOU'RE ALL ABOUT
GIVING A LITTLE GRACE,
WHEREVER IT'S NEEDED MOST.

IT'S HARD TO STAY
DISCOURAGED
FOR LONG
AROUND SOMEONE
LIKE YOU!

Have I not commanded you?
Be strong and courageous.
Do not be afraid; do not be discouraged,
for the Lord your God
will be with you wherever you go.

JOSHUA 1:9

YOU'RE SOMEONE
PEOPLE TRUST...
TO DO WHAT YOU SAY,
TO SAY WHAT YOU MEAN,
TO BE THERE WHEN
THEY NEED YOU.

BECAUSE OF YOUR FAITH
AND THE WAY YOU'RE ALWAYS
SO REAL WITH PEOPLE,
GOD'S MORE REAL TO THEM, TOO.

*Hope you know
what a beautiful thing that is.*

Let your light shine before others,
that they may see your good deeds
and glorify your Father in heaven.

MATTHEW 5:16

THERE'S NOTHING
"HOLIER THAN THOU"
ABOUT YOU.

YOUR BRAVE, FAITHFUL SPIRIT SAYS,

"LOOK OUT, WORLD.
I'VE GOT BACKUP."

Love YOUR GENTLE SOUL...
YOUR PEACEFUL POINT OF VIEW.

Blessed are the peacemakers,
for they will be called children of God.

MATTHEW 5:9

YOU MIGHT NOT HAVE
ACTUAL SUPERPOWERS,
BUT YOU'VE GOT
GOD'S POWER IN YOU,
AND THAT'S EVEN BETTER.

I AM SO GIVING THANKS
FOR EVERYTHING ABOUT YOU!

Rejoice always, pray continually,
give thanks in all circumstances; for this
is God's will for you in Jesus Christ.

1 THESSALONIANS 5:16–18

EVERYONE YOU MEET
GETS YOUR BEST...
AND WALKS AWAY
A LITTLE MORE BLESSED.

YOUR **LAUGHTER** IS A **JOYFUL** THING, JUST THE KIND OF **GIFT** I NEED NOW AND THEN.

IT'S A LIFE-AFFIRMING BLESSING...AND SO ARE YOU!

He will yet fill your mouth with laughter
and your lips with shouts of joy.

JOB 8:21

YOU HELP OTHERS BELIEVE
THAT ANYTHING IS POSSIBLE—
THAT EVERYTHING IS PRAY-ABLE!

YOU'VE GOT
THE WHOLE
GOLDEN RULE
THING DOWN.

Do to others as you would have them do to you.

LUKE 6:31

YOU'RE SO OPEN
AND ACCEPTING...
ENCOURAGEMENT
MUST BE YOUR
SPIRITUAL GIFT!

Therefore encourage one another and build each other up.

1 THESSALONIANS 5:11

GENEROSITY
IS YOUR DEFAULT MODE, YOUR
UPBEAT ATTITUDE
AN EVERYDAY THING. YOU'RE A
GOD-MADE
GIVER OF GOODNESS,
plain and simple.

God loves a cheerful giver.

2 CORINTHIANS 9:7

LOVE PEOPLE FIRST.
ASK QUESTIONS LATER.
JUDGE NEVER.

That's how you roll.

YOU DON'T PRETEND
TO HAVE ALL THE ANSWERS.
BUT YOU KNOW WHO TO GO TO
WITH EVERY QUESTION.

Trust in the Lord with all your heart
and lean not on your own understanding;
in all your ways submit to him,
and he will make your paths straight.

PROVERBS 3:5–6

YOU TREAT
EVERYONE
LIKE THE
ANGELS
THEY JUST MIGHT BE.

WHEN IT COMES TO
FRUITS OF THE SPIRIT,
YOU'VE GOT A
BUMPER CROP.

The fruit of the Spirit is love, joy, peace, forbearance, kindness, goodness, faithfulness, gentleness, and self-control.

GALATIANS 5:22-23

YOU REALLY TAKE THAT
"LOVE THY NEIGHBOR"
ATTITUDE TO HEART.

IN THIS "LOOK AT ME" WORLD, YOU'RE SOMEONE WHO DOESN'T MAKE A BIG DEAL OUT OF THE GOOD THAT YOU DO. **YOU JUST QUIETLY DO IT.**

What does the LORD require of you?
To act justly and to love mercy
and to walk humbly with your God.

MICAH 6:8

THERE'S NO ONE BETTER
TO BELIEVE WITH,
SHARE DOUBTS WITH,
PRAY HARD WITH,
OR CELEBRATE LIFE WITH
than you.

YOU'VE DONE
A LOT OF FAVORS
AND GONE
A LOT
OF EXTRA MILES.

If anyone forces you to go one mile,
go with them two miles.

MATTHEW 5:41

GOD MEANT FOR US
TO SHINE OUR LIGHT,
BUT I THINK HE GAVE YOU
EXTRA WATTAGE.

I'm so grateful for all the ways
you brighten my life.

IF GOD GAVE OUT
REPORT CARDS,
"SHARES WELL WITH OTHERS"
WOULD SURELY
BE ON YOURS.

Do not forget to do good and to share with others,
for with such sacrifices God is pleased.

HEBREWS 13:16

WITH SOMEONE LIKE YOU IN MY LIFE, I FEEL LIKE GOD IS SPOILING ME A LITTLE.

YOU ACCOMPLISH A LOT,
NOT BY BEING BUSY EVERY MINUTE,
BUT BY TAKING TIME OUT
TO JUST BE STILL
IN GOD'S PRESENCE.

Be still before the LORD
and wait patiently for him.

PSALM 37:7-9

YOU PUT YOUR HEART
INTO WORKING
TO MAKE THINGS RIGHT—
NOT INTO POINTING OUT
WHAT'S WRONG.

The world thanks you.
God thanks you.

NOT ONLY DO YOU
GET ALONG WITH EVERYONE,
YOU BRING PEOPLE TOGETHER...
IN A WAY THAT SURELY
MUST BE A GOD THING.

If it is possible, as far as it depends on you,
live at peace with everyone.

ROMANS 12:18

I DON'T ALWAYS KNOW
HOW MY PRAYERS
WILL BE ANSWERED.
BUT I'VE NOTICED THAT
YOUR HELPING HANDS
ARE ONE OF THE NICEST WAYS.

YOU HAVE A WONDERFUL

ATTITUDE OF GRATITUDE.

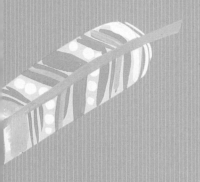

YOU NOT ONLY FORGIVE,
YOU FORGET.
GRUDGES DON'T STAND A CHANCE
IN A HEART LIKE YOURS!

Forgive as the LORD forgave you.

COLOSSIANS 3:13

IT'S NICE TO HAVE SOMEONE WHO'S ON THE SAME JOURNEY, LEARNING AND GROWING, QUESTIONING AND SEEKING.

THANKS
FOR EVERY TIME
YOU'VE SHARED
THE FIRST CHOICE,
THE BIGGER HALF,
OR THE BETTER PART
OF SOMETHING WITH ME.

Be devoted to one another in love.
Honor one another above yourselves.

ROMANS 12:10

Don't ever change…
I like you just the way God made you.

IF YOU HAVE ENJOYED THIS BOOK
OR IT HAS TOUCHED YOUR LIFE IN SOME WAY,
WE WOULD LOVE TO HEAR FROM YOU.

Please send your comments to:
Hallmark Book Feedback
P.O. Box 419034
Mail Drop 100
Kansas City, MO 64141

Or e-mail us at:
booknotes@hallmark.com